J oy can sometimes be elusive and other times contagious. When we think about joy, we tend to visualize excitement or even ecstasy, but the true emotion is a much quieter, richer feeling of peace and contentment. It's simple happiness rather than something frantic and over-the-top. In our busy, fast-paced world it's sometimes difficult to slow down and experience the pleasure of joyfulness. It's a matter of learning how to recognize it and tapping into it. If you find yourself struggling to identify joy in your life, don't worry, you're not alone. Sometimes it simply takes a switch in perspective to notice the things for which you can be joyful. It may be the act of identifying the positives in your life rather than focusing on the negatives. Or mindfully taking the time to seek out fun activities, interesting places, and people who bring joy to your life: focusing on the delicious sense of peaceful happiness you feel in their presence. Slow yourself down and revel in those sudden feelings of complete contentment that we all unexpectedly experience from time to time. Think about what makes you feel joy and make sure you incorporate those things into your life. Ponder, reflect, and drink in your joy because when you are in a joyful state, feeling a sense that all is well, your mind and body can't help but be at ease and feel good.

VISUALIZE A LIFE IN WHICH
YOU AWAKEN EACH MORNING TO
GREET THE DAY WITH A SMILE
BECAUSE YOU KNOW GOOD THINGS
WILL HAPPEN TO YOU!

GET ENOUGH SLEEP! IT'S IMPORTANT TO GIVE
YOURSELF THE TIME YOU NEED SO YOUR BRAIN
AND BODY WILL FUNCTION AT THEIR HIGHEST
POSSIBLE LEVELS.

BE A BLESSING TO THOSE AROUND YOU WITH YOUR WORDS. IT'S AS SIMPLE AS SPEAKING KIND WORDS TO ONE ANOTHER. ACKNOWLEDGE THOSE WHO ARE DEAREST TO YOU BY SAYING, "I BELIEVE IN YOU. YOU'RE BEAUTIFUL. I APPRECIATE YOU. THANK YOU FOR BEING YOU AND LOVING ME."

TALK TO DIFFERENT PEOPLE AND NOTICE WHAT YOU ENJOY ABOUT THE ENCOUNTERS.

PAY ATTENTION TO
THE POSITIVE THINGS
AROUND YOU.

NOTICE WHAT MAKES YOU
FEEL HAPPY AND UPLIFTED.

FEEL FAMILIAR IN YOUR JOY AND
YOUR POSITIVE EXPECTATIONS.

YOU ARE HERE TO BE
A STRONG, COMPETENT,
JOYFUL PERSON WHO
HAS A GREATER PURPOSE.

ONCE YOUR MIND IS FREE FROM FOCUSING
ON FEAR, IT WILL BE AVAILABLE TO
FOCUS ON POSITIVE EMOTIONS, LIKE JOY.

BEING PRESENT IN THE MOMENT
STOPS NEGATIVE, RUMINATING
THOUGHTS FROM SUCKING AWAY
YOUR JOYFULNESS AND BECOMING
YOUR REALITY.

DON'T CONFUSE WHAT
COULD HAPPEN WITH WHAT
IS. FIND YOUR JOYFULNESS
IN THE MOMENT.

THREE IMPORTANT THINGS TO DO: (1) EAT BREAKFAST, (2) DRINK WATER, (3) EXERCISE. EVEN IF YOU DO NOTHING ELSE, THOSE THREE HABITS WILL HAVE A PROFOUND EFFECT ON TURNING YOUR LIFE AROUND.

TAKE NOTE OF WHAT YOU'RE GOOD AT AND ALLOW YOURSELF TO FEEL SATISFACTION FROM THAT FACT.

HAVING FRIENDSHIPS AND RICH PERSONAL RELATIONSHIPS ARE KEYS TO LIVING A JOYFUL LIFE.

ACTIVELY SEEK OUT WHAT BRINGS YOU PEACEFUL PLEASURES.

NOURISH YOURSELF. DO SOMETHING YOU TRULY ENJOY.

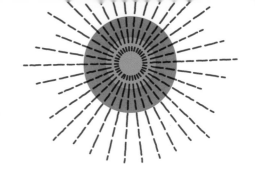

JOY ISN'T NECESSARILY A THRILLING ROLLER COASTER RIDE; IT CAN BE PEACEFUL, CALM WATERS.

LOOK AT YOURSELF AND MAKE SURE YOU ARE CHAMPIONING THE PEOPLE WHO ARE CLOSE TO YOU.

CHAPTER 2

LIVING A PURPOSEFUL, ABUNDANT LIFE (IS YOUR GLASS HALF-FULL?)

DO YOU VIEW YOUR
WORLD THROUGH THE
LENS OF ABUNDANCE
OR SCARCITY?

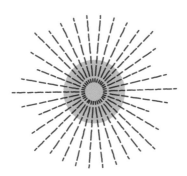

Living out your life's purpose doesn't prevent obstacles, difficulties, and occasional dead ends from happening. But viewing your life through the lens of abundance and knowing your purpose allows you to focus on your personal goals, even while you're navigating the ins and outs of everyday life. Seeing your life this way is more than just defining your life's goals. It's bigger than that. *Purpose* is the umbrella of life-meaning under which you live. In fact, it's the very reason you exist. And the lens of *abundance* is a way of looking at and appreciating all the blessings you have in your life—many of which you may never even think about, like clean water to drink and a warm bed to snuggle into on a cold night.

No matter what defines your purpose, you are called to action: to grow, become more self-aware, to work toward living out this purposeful life. Knowing your purpose is important because it will stop you from detouring on your life's path and allowing whimsy and impulsiveness to steer you. Knowing your calling allows you to live a deeper, richer, more meaningful life.

MONEY DOES NOT INCREASE
OR DECREASE A PERSON'S VALUE,
AND OUR VIEW OF SUCCESS
SHOULD HAVE LESS TO DO WITH
THE AMOUNT OF CASH A PERSON
HAS THAN WITH WHAT HE OR SHE
DOES WITH WHAT THEY HAVE.

DON'T CARRY YOUR DISAPPOINTMENTS ON
YOUR SHOULDERS. THEY'LL WEIGH YOU DOWN.
INSTEAD, FOCUS ON THE POSITIVES BECAUSE
THAT IS WHERE YOU'LL FIND YOUR JOY.

"THE MYSTERY OF HUMAN EXISTENCE LIES
NOT IN JUST STAYING ALIVE, BUT IN FINDING
SOMETHING TO LIVE FOR."

                              -FYODOR DOSTOYEVSKY

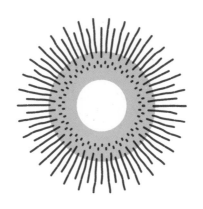

FOR ME, WHEN I AM NOT LIVING OUT MY
LIFE'S PURPOSE, I FEEL A TERRIBLE LACK
OF PEACE, LIKE I'VE LOST MY WAY, AND
I BECOME STRESSED OUT BOTH PHYSICALLY
AND EMOTIONALLY.

VIEW LIFE'S CIRCUMSTANCES
THROUGH A LENS OF ABUNDANCE.
IT'S ALL ABOUT THE MINDSET.

LIFE IS A WORK IN PROGRESS.

EMBRACE WHAT IT MEANS TO BE A PERSON OF VITALITY AND AUTHENTICITY. IT IS NOT ABOUT TRYING TO OUTDO THOSE WHOM YOU LOOK UP TO, OR EXCEEDING OTHERS IN HOW MUCH MONEY, POWER, STATUS, OR DESIRABLE QUALITIES THEY HAVE. IT'S ABOUT BEING THE BEST VERSION OF YOURSELF.

THINK OF YOUR MINDSET AS A BANK ACCOUNT
AND ASK YOURSELF HOW MANY POSITIVE AND
EMPOWERING THOUGHTS YOU ARE DEPOSITING
EACH DAY.

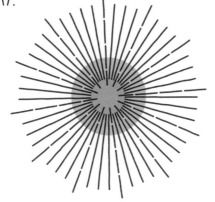

STOP YOURSELF FROM NEGATIVE THINKING,
COMPLAINING, TIME-WASTING ACTIVITIES,
PROCRASTINATION, ANGST, FRUSTRATION,
TEARING OTHERS DOWN, TEARING YOURSELF
DOWN, GOSSIP, AND OTHER NEGATIVE BEHAVIORS.

ARE YOU FOCUSING
ON A MENTALITY
OF SCARCITY INSTEAD
OF ABUNDANCE?
IF SO, IT'S TIME TO
TURN THAT AROUND

THE KEY IS TO MAINTAIN A POSITIVE OUTLOOK. IT'S NOT ALWAYS EASY, BUT THERE ARE VERY SPECIFIC ACTIONS YOU CAN TAKE TO KEEP YOURSELF FOCUSED AND IN A MINDSET OF ABUNDANCE.

KEEP IN MIND THAT ABUNDANCE IS MORE THAN JUST MONETARY RICHES.

MOVING YOUR FOCUS FROM THE NEGATIVE TO THE POSITIVE TAKES PURPOSEFUL ACTION ON YOUR PART.

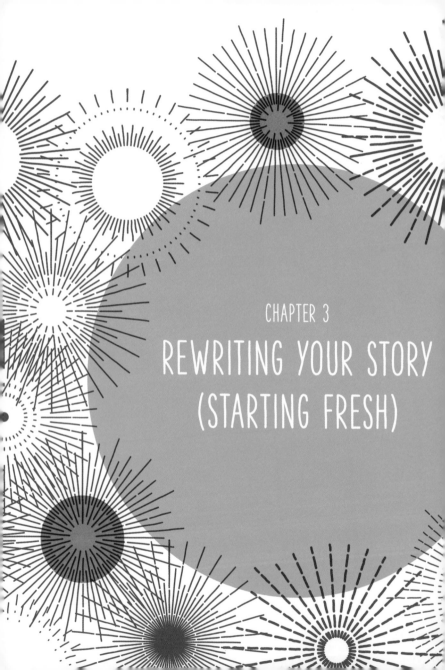

CHAPTER 3

REWRITING YOUR STORY (STARTING FRESH)

WHEN YOU VIEW YOURSELF
THROUGH THE LENS OF
"WORTHINESS" THE WORLD
LOOKS DIFFERENT. IT LOOKS
LIKE SOMEPLACE YOU
CAN FIND SUCCESS AND
ACCOMPLISH YOUR DREAMS.

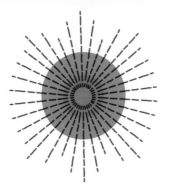

Is your old story holding you back? How you are living now is not how your story ends. Your current situation is a temporary condition. The best is yet to be! The story of the past can't be rewritten, but the pages going forward are blank. Begin to write your story by taking a hard look at how you spend the hours of your day, because no matter what your intentions are, how you spend your time has a profound influence on your life. If you do need to make significant changes in your life in order to achieve happiness, then it's time to really think about that. What should you change? Begin to ponder it.

Fear is a very real emotion when the desire to make changes arises. Thoughts of self-defeat come pouring in like a tidal wave. Feelings of inadequacy come to the surface. Sometimes these fears and feelings of inadequacy are so overwhelming you choose to cling on to the world you know even if it's unsatisfying. At least it's known, right? You have to stop that kind of defeatist thinking!

Take some time and question your fears. Unpack them one by one, with question after question, and follow your questions to their conclusion. You will most likely see that your fears are unwarranted and keeping you from achieving your goals. It's time to change your "I can't" to "I can." It simply takes some rewriting.

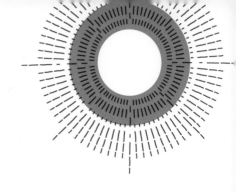

CHANGE MAY TAKE SOME
COURAGE, ENCOURAGEMENT,
AND TENACITY. REMEMBER
THOUGH, THAT YOU CAN DO IT!

WE ALL HAVE OUR STORIES. . . BUT HOW YOU
WRITE YOURS IS WHAT COUNTS. SEPARATE
WHATEVER YOUR PAST CIRCUMSTANCES WERE
FROM WHERE YOU ARE RIGHT NOW. IT'S TIME
TO CREATE THE STORY YOU WILL BE PROUD
OF AND FULFILLED BY.

I CAN SEE IN MYSELF WHAT
MY FUTURE WILL BE.

HAVE COURAGE AND
TAKE ACTION IN
SPITE OF FEARS.

INCONVENIENCE YOURSELF IF
YOU WANT CHANGE.

DON'T ARGUE ABOUT
WHAT IT TAKES.

BE WILLING TO WORK
THROUGH FEARS THAT ARISE.

BE OPEN TO LEARNING
FROM OTHERS.

CONVICTION AND CONVENIENCE DO NOT LIVE IN THE SAME SPACE.

YOUR CONVICTION HAS TO COST YOU SOMETHING. WHAT ARE YOU WILLING TO BE INCONVENIENCED BY TO GET WHERE YOU'RE DESTINED TO BE? GET OUT OF "COMFORTABLE."

DISMISS WHAT YOU HAVE ALLOWED TO GET IN THE WAY OF CHANGE.

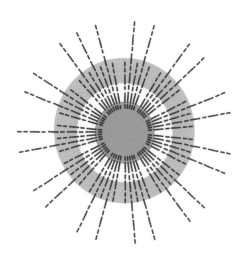

MAKE GOOD USE OF YOUR TIME!

DON'T ALLOW OTHERS
TO CONTROL YOUR
DECISIONS, FEELINGS,
AND MIND-SET. YOU
ARE THE WRITER
OF THE SCRIPT OF
YOUR LIFE.

TAKE STEPS OF FAITH
INSTEAD OF STANDING
PARALYZED IN YOUR
PAST STORY.

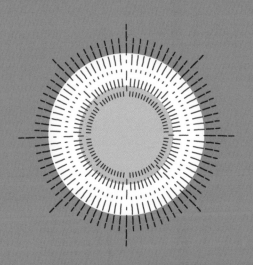

BE OK WITH NOT KNOWING THE
ANSWERS ALL THE TIME. IT'S A
LIFE IN PROGRESS.

DON'T GIVE UP ON YOURSELF, BUT SURRENDER
TO THE PROCESS.

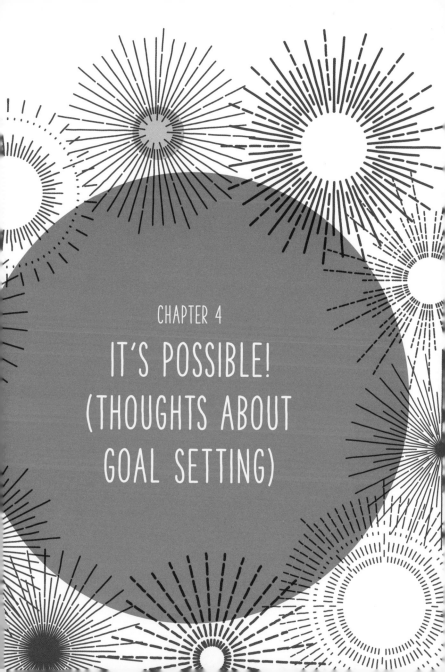

CHAPTER 4

IT'S POSSIBLE!
(THOUGHTS ABOUT
GOAL SETTING)

ANY SMALL THING
YOU DO TO REACH
YOUR PERSONAL
GOALS WILL KEEP
YOU MOVING IN A
POSITIVE DIRECTION.

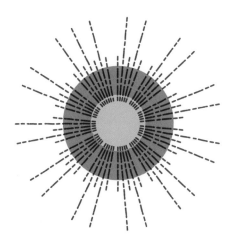

Take a step back, examine your life, and make sure you're not just going through the motions. Do things that matter to you. Do what's important to live a life you can be proud of.

It's easy to slip into the habit of talking yourself out of changes you know you should make. It's time to break that pattern. You have to allow yourself to pay attention to the emotional side of your logic as well as the intellectual side, and open yourself up to operating from your heart, as well as your head. I'm not advocating that you stop thinking, but simply that you stop overanalyzing the changes you know you need to make. Don't talk yourself out of what you want and need to do. Sometimes you need to take a leap.

If you're going to make it, you'll need to have faith. In fact, when you begin your transformation all odds may be against you, but that is where the magic can happen. See the harvest in the midst of famine. Know in your heart that you may not understand it all, but you're still going to take steps forward in faith.

REALIZE HOW MUCH YOU
CAN ACCOMPLISH.

THE LONGEST JOURNEYS STILL
BEGIN WITH ONE STEP.

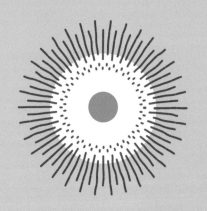

BE BRAVE.

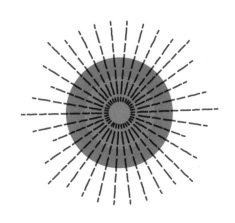

STOP COMPARING AND
COMPLAINING. TAKE
RESPONSIBILITY AND GET
IT DONE.

BE THE EXAMPLE OF WHAT
IS POSSIBLE.

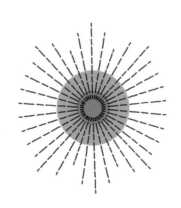

WHAT ARE YOU DOING WELL AND WHAT NEEDS TO CHANGE?

FOCUS ON WHAT YOU HAVE AND ASK YOURSELF HOW YOU CAN ADD WHAT YOU WANT.

EVERY ACTION YOU MAKE
IN LIFE CAUSES A CHAIN OF
CONSEQUENCES, SO MAKE SURE
YOUR ACTIONS ARE MOVING YOU
IN THE DIRECTION YOU WANT.

TAKE FEAR OUT OF
THE EQUATION.

REMEMBER YOUR OVERARCHING PURPOSE.

IF YOUR TRUE PURPOSE IS SOMETHING LARGER
THAN YOURSELF, IT KEEPS THE SMALLER THINGS
IN LIFE-THINGS THAT CAN SEEM SO HUGE IN
THE MOMENT-IN PERSPECTIVE.

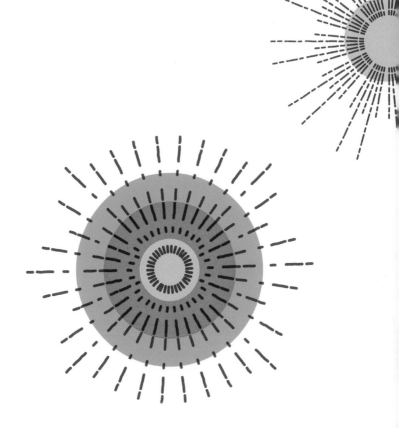

MAKE A COMMITMENT.

FERTILIZE YOUR BRAIN WITH
POSITIVE MESSAGES EVERY DAY.

EVEN SLOW PROGRESS
IS PROGRESS.

SET YOUR INTENTION
FOR THE DAY AS
SOON AS YOUR FEET
HIT THE FLOOR.

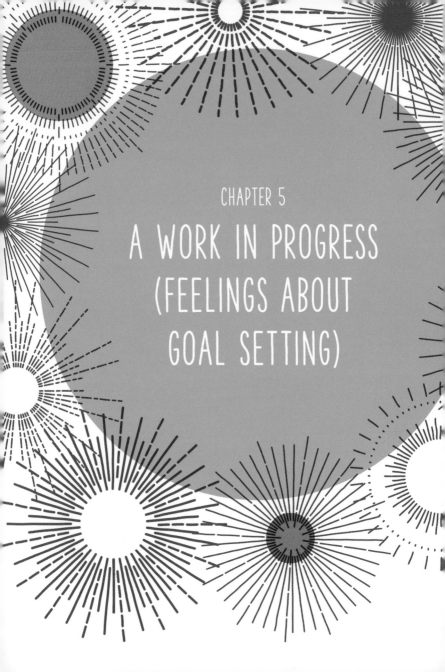

CHAPTER 5

A WORK IN PROGRESS (FEELINGS ABOUT GOAL SETTING)

NO MATTER OUR
THOUGHTS, OUR
ACTIONS DEFINE US.

Take a look at where you are with regards to your dreams and desires and then map out where you want to be. You may be very far away or just a few simple steps from attaining what you're visualizing, but either way, things are changing. And whether the transformation is subtle or radical, you should feel excited during the journey. If that hasn't been the case so far, it may be that you're following the wrong road. Perhaps you're working towards a dream that someone *else* wants you to achieve, instead of doing what you want to do. Maybe you're just going along with a particular plan for your life because you feel you have to.

Take a moment to observe your feelings about the dreams you are pursuing. If you noticed that the thought of working towards achieving them leaves you feeling unenthusiastic, then that particular goal may be coming from the head (I *should* do) rather than the heart (I *want* to do). A head-based goal is derived from a place of proving something to someone or seeking it out because it's "the right thing to accomplish" based on your family's or society's expectations. A heart-based goal makes you feel good, full of expectation and hope. Those are the personal goals you should be working on because if your life is a work in progress, you want to make sure your progress takes you where you want to go.

ASK YOURSELF THE FOLLOWING: WHAT RESULTS
DO I WANT? WHAT DO I WANT TO ACHIEVE?

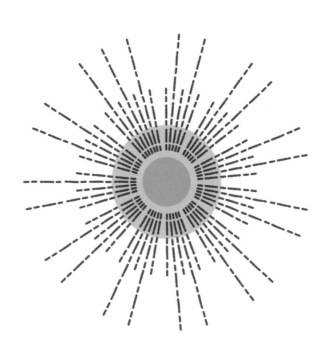

TRANSFORMATION IS NOT
EASY, BUT IT IS WORTH
IT. IT'S ABOUT STAYING
STRONG FOR THE LONG
HAUL. IT'S THE OLD ADAGE
THAT YOU CAN'T JUST
TALK THE TALK, YOU HAVE
TO WALK THE WALK.

WE ARE ALL IN THE DRIVER'S SEAT OF OUR
OWN DESTINY. EACH DECISION WE MAKE,
WHETHER SMALL OR LARGE, HAS A RIPPLE
EFFECT IN OUR LIVES. EACH RADIATES CHANGE.

IT'S EASY TO FORGET THAT
NO MATTER WHAT SITUATION
WE'RE IN, THERE IS ALWAYS
A CHOICE ABOUT HOW WE
WANT TO PROCEED.

THINK ABOUT YOUR
GOALS AND LOOK AT
THEM OFTEN TO KEEP
YOURSELF ON TRACK.

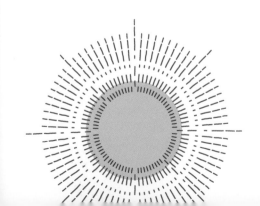

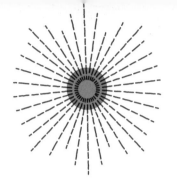

NO MATTER WHERE YOU ARE ON LIFE'S JOURNEY, THERE ARE BETTER THINGS WAITING FOR YOU IN YOUR FUTURE.

PLAN FOR YOUR FUTURE. KNOW WHERE YOU'RE GOING AND COMMIT TO GETTING THERE.

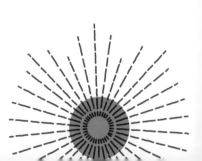

THINK ABOUT WHICH QUALITIES
YOU NEED TO FURTHER DEVELOP
IN YOURSELF.

BECOME A SOLUTION-
ORIENTED PERSON.

EACH TIME YOU THINK "I CAN'T"
THINK OF ONE SOLUTION TO THE
PROBLEM AT HAND. JUST ONE.

TAKE CHARGE, TAKE
SMALL STEPS, AND
EVENTUALLY THINGS
YOU BELIEVED WEREN'T
POSSIBLE WILL HAPPEN.

IT TAKES WORK ON MULTIPLE LEVELS TO ACHIEVE AND CONTINUE ACHIEVING.

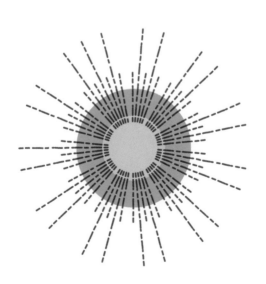

DON'T DESPAIR, BECAUSE THERE IS
SATISFACTION IN WORKING TOWARDS YOUR
GOALS, EVEN IF YOU HAVE TO SET ASIDE SOME
THINGS YOU ENJOY WHILE YOU DO.

SURROUND YOURSELF WITH
FRIENDS AND PEOPLE WHO
INSPIRE YOU.

TAKE A MOMENT TO BASK IN THE
HAPPINESS THAT RECOGNITION
BRINGS AND RECEIVE IT WITH
UTMOST APPRECIATION.

THE INTENTIONS YOU SET FOR YOUR LIFE ARE
TREMENDOUSLY INFLUENTIAL ON THE PERSON
YOU WANT TO BECOME. HOW YOU ACT DEPENDS
UPON WHAT YOUR INTENTIONS ARE.

SETTING GOALS AND THINKING
THROUGH YOUR INTENTIONS ARE
POWERFUL WAYS TO STRENGTHEN
THE UNDERSTANDING OF EXACTLY
WHAT YOU PLAN TO ACHIEVE
AT THE END OF YOUR PERSONAL
JOURNEY.

WHEN THINKING ABOUT HOW TO ACHIEVE THE
NEXT STEP ON THE JOURNEY TO YOUR GOALS,
ASK YOURSELF THIS: HOW DO I WANT TO FEEL
BEFORE, DURING, AND AFTER?

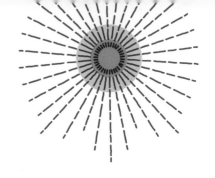

CREATE A LIST OF THINGS YOU DID TODAY THAT
LED TOWARD AN ACHIEVEMENT, SOMETHING
YOU CAN ACTUALLY POINT TO. THEN TELL
YOURSELF, "I DID THIS! IT WAS IMPORTANT TO
ME AND I ACHIEVED MY PERSONAL GOAL."

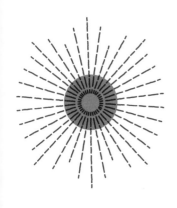

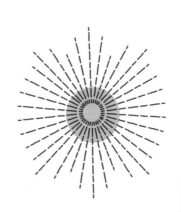

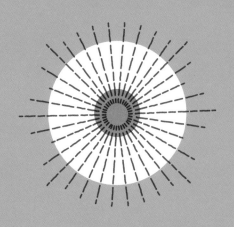

NOTE ALL THE SUCCESSES ALONG
THE WAY TO YOUR END GOAL
AND ONCE YOU'VE COMPLETED
IT, WRITE DOWN THE FACT
THAT YOU'VE ACHIEVED YOUR
OBJECTIVE AND ACKNOWLEDGE
A JOB WELL-DONE.

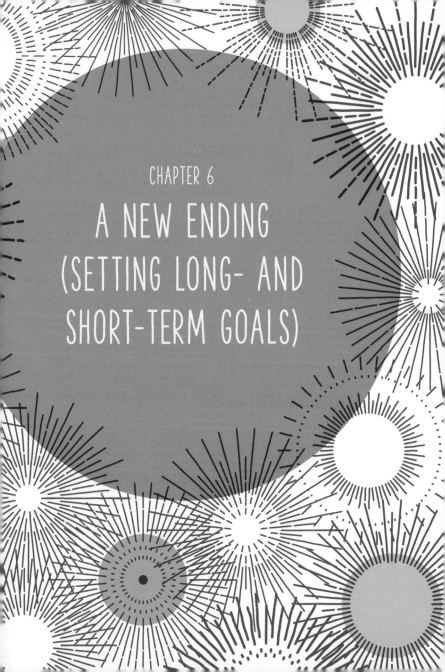

CHAPTER 6

A NEW ENDING (SETTING LONG- AND SHORT-TERM GOALS)

TAKE RESPONSIBILITY
FOR YOUR DESTINY.

Transformation begins by setting clear, achievable goals. Make some large, long-term goals and some smaller, easily measured goals that you can achieve en route to accomplishing your long-term goals. Take pride in achieving the smaller goals and know that with each small goal you achieve, you are gaining strength and working towards transformation. Don't worry about failures along the way. They're simply setbacks. After all, we all fail sometimes, but it's what you do with failure that counts. Don't allow it to define you. Think of it as character building. All experiences add to your strength. You'll see that you can fail and live through it. You can shake it off and keep moving forward. Learn from it. You can use it to remind yourself what *not* to do the next time. Accept the challenge to transform yourself *every day*. Keep saying yes. Understand that even though you may be tired, in pain, too short, overweight, or broke, you can still live out your goals, even if they are achieved one baby step at a time.

EVERY CHOICE YOU MAKE DEFINES WHO YOU ARE BECOMING. BE DILIGENT ABOUT THOSE CHOICES.

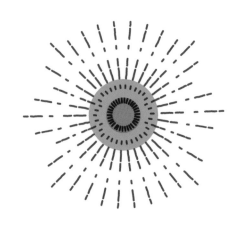

IN ORDER TO ACHIEVE MOST THINGS
IN LIFE, YOU HAVE TO FOCUS ON THE
LONG-TERM GOAL AND PUT IN THE
EFFORT REQUIRED TO GIVE YOURSELF
ACCESS TO LIFE'S GREATEST
REWARDS. VALUE THAT ARRIVES IN
AN INSTANT IS PROBABLY GOING TO
BE GONE IN AN INSTANT. VALUE THAT
TAKES TIME AND COMMITMENT TO
CREATE WILL ENRICH YOUR LIFE FAR
INTO THE FUTURE.

BE SELF-INSPIRED AND KNOW YOU CAN DO
WHAT YOU WANT TO DO.

CREATE SHORT-TERM GOALS
THAT HELP YOU REACH YOUR
LONG-TERM GOALS.

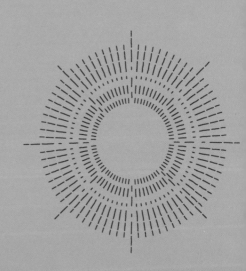

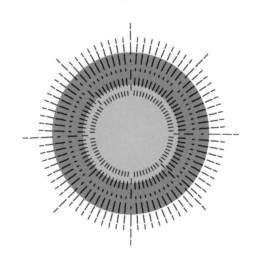

FREE YOURSELF
FROM WHAT OTHERS
THINK ABOUT YOU.

YOUR ABILITY TO SEE YOURSELF
CLEARLY IS AN OPPORTUNITY
TO LEARN AND RETHINK YOUR
CURRENT COURSE OF EXECUTION.
KNOWING YOUR STRENGTHS AND
WEAKNESSES WILL HELP YOU
DETERMINE THE CHANGES YOU
NEED TO MAKE TO BECOME THE
PERSON YOU WANT TO BE.

PERSEVERANCE, STRENGTH, AND EXCITEMENT ARE KEY ELEMENTS TO ACHIEVING SUCCESS.

WHEN I'M DOING SOMETHING BIG, I LEARN AND GROW.

DARE TO PLAY BIG!

MAKE SURE YOU'RE SOMEONE YOU WANT TO BE.

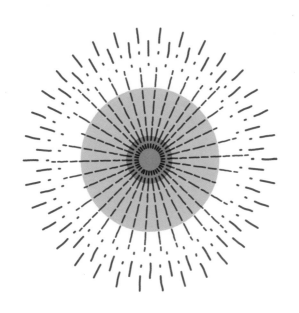

FOCUS ON THE END GOAL. BE STRONG AND RESPONSIBLE FOR YOUR OWN ACTIONS.

BIG DREAMS AND GOALS ARE
ACHIEVED NOT BY DOING
EVERYTHING AT ONCE, BUT
BY PURPOSEFULLY WORKING
TOWARDS YOUR GOALS ONE STEP
AT A TIME.

FOCUS ON WHAT IS GOING WELL IN YOUR LIFE.
NOTE THE GOALS YOU HAVE ACHIEVED OR ARE
ACTIVELY WORKING TOWARDS ACCOMPLISHING.

MAKE SURE EVERYBODY IN YOUR "BOAT" IS ROWING (SUPPORTING AND LOVING YOUR PATH IN LIFE), NOT DRILLING HOLES WHEN YOU'RE NOT LOOKING.

"PERSEVERANCE IS NOT
A LONG RACE. IT'S MANY
SHORT RACES RUN ONE
AFTER ANOTHER."
                    -WALTER ELLIOT

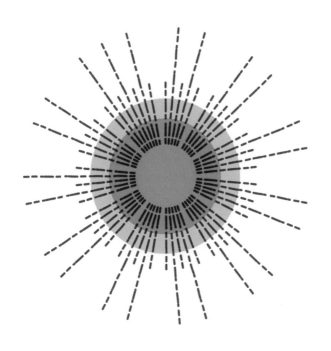

EVERY SMALL SUCCESS IS PURE FUEL. YOUR
EXCITEMENT, INTELLIGENCE, AND THE AWARENESS
THAT YOU CAN LIVE THE LIFE YOU DREAM OF
FUELS THE HOPE YOU NEED TO PERSEVERE.

CHAPTER 7

TEMPORARY SETBACKS (KEEPING GOING!)

BE WILLING TO GET
BRUISED SHINS AND
SKINNED KNEES AS
YOU FALL DOWN
AND BUMP INTO
ROADBLOCKS...AND
THEN GET BACK UP.

Everyone has experienced rejection. It can be painful, but it's important to remember that rejection is not failure. Rejection is an emotional sting that may come up on your path to change. Any form of rejection can hurt, and it might make you wonder why you are doing what you are doing. It can put you in the *temporarily defeated* zone of life. If that's where you are, it's time for a mind-set shift. If you view rejection as failure, it will absolutely freeze you in place. Don't allow that to be the case. So what to do if your dream doesn't come true? When that happens, it's time to ask yourself this important question: *Now what?* The answer is *keep moving forward* because there are usually several ways to achieve your goals. One unexpected twist in the road doesn't mean that you will never arrive at your desired destination. Don't give up! Acknowledge the setback as just that and keep going.

BEING IN ACHIEVEMENT
MODE WILL NATURALLY
SHIFT YOUR ATTITUDE
ABOUT PROBLEMS,
ENABLING YOU TO SEE
THEM AS OPPORTUNITIES
TO BE BETTER INSTEAD OF
AS FAILURES.

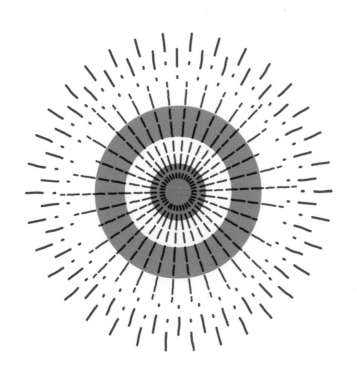

TAKE SOME QUIET TIME EACH DAY TO
RECONNECT WITH YOURSELF AND YOUR GOALS.

NOTICE IF DISTRACTIONS ARE LURING YOU OFF YOUR PATH.

TAKE NOTE OF WHAT IS DISTRACTING YOU
FROM FULFILLING YOUR GOALS AND DESIRES.

STAYING IN A POSITIVE-INTENTION STATE WILL
BREED INSPIRATION, EXCITEMENT, AND HOPE,
WHICH WILL MOVE YOU OUT OF THE STUCK
STATE AND INTO ONE OF CREATIVE POWER
AND ACCOMPLISHMENT.

IT'S IMPORTANT THAT YOU DON'T
ASSUME YOU'VE BEEN DEFEATED
IN YOUR EFFORTS BECAUSE
THINGS ARE NOT HAPPENING AS
QUICKLY AS YOU'D LIKE.

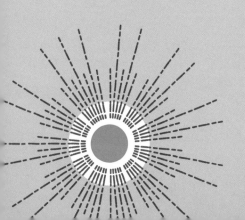

REMEMBER THIS: IF SOMETHING DOESN'T HAPPEN IMMEDIATELY, DON'T AUTOMATICALLY THINK YOU'VE FAILED. FAST RESULTS DON'T ALWAYS POINT TO SUCCESS.

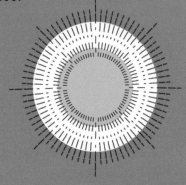

FAILURE IS A PART OF LIFE. IT'S HOW QUICKLY YOU RECOVER (LEARN FROM YOUR MISTAKES) THAT SHOWS YOUR STRENGTH.

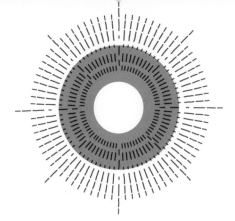

BE OPEN ABOUT YOUR STRUGGLES
SO THAT OTHERS WILL FEEL
THAT THEY, TOO, CAN BE
OPEN ABOUT THEIRS. THAT'S
WHEN MUTUAL SUPPORT AND
INSPIRATION CAN HAPPEN.

GETTING OUT OF A MEDIOCRE MIND-SET TAKES GUTS AND RISK OF REJECTION, BUT IT'S WORTH IT.

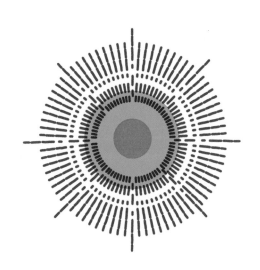

IF YOU START FORWARD ON YOUR JOURNEY
WITH A HOPEFUL, POSITIVE ATTITUDE, EVEN
THOUGH YOU ARE GOING TO FACE CHALLENGES,
YOU WILL PREVAIL. IT DOESN'T MEAN THAT
EVERYTHING WILL MAGICALLY FALL INTO
PLACE. IT DOESN'T EVEN MEAN YOU WILL
ABSOLUTELY ACHIEVE WHAT YOU SET OUT
TO ACCOMPLISH; BUT YOU WILL BE MOVING
TOWARDS YOUR GOAL.

ALONG THE WAY, YOU WILL HAVE SETBACKS.
YOU WILL STUMBLE AND FALL. DON'T LET
THAT DEFINE YOU. THAT DOESN'T MAKE YOU A
FAILURE, IT SIMPLY MAKES YOU HUMAN.

IF YOU THINK OF DIFFICULTIES AS EXCITING CHALLENGES, THEN YOU WILL HAVE A DIFFERENT MIND-SET TOWARDS THEM. THEY ARE NOT DEFEATS, BUT SIMPLY SOMETHING TO FIGURE OUT AND OVERCOME.

REJECTION IS NOT FAILURE.

IF SOMETHING YOU HAVE BEEN STRIVING FOR
IS NOT GOING TO HAPPEN, ALLOW YOURSELF
TO MOVE ON AND UNDERSTAND THAT YOU CAN
BE HAPPY NO MATTER WHAT PATH YOU TAKE.
FIGURE OUT YOUR HAPPINESS WHERE YOU ARE.

FEAR IS NOT A FACT. IT'S A FEELING.

DON'T DEFINE YOURSELF
AS A FAILURE BECAUSE
YOU HAVEN'T YET MADE
IT TO YOUR PLANNED
DESTINATION. REVEL IN
THE BEAUTY OF WHERE
YOU ARE.

CHRISTINE HARDY is the author of *Unlock Your Victory Code: The Key to Hope, Perseverance and Triumph*. She is a Certified Nutrition Educator with a master's degree in nutrition. She has worked as a clinical counselor for young teenagers with behavioral and drug-dependency issues and has worked with patients with cancer, diabetes, osteoporosis, and endocrine disorders to create specialized nutritional programs to promote healing and health.

Her purpose is to help people live long, joyful lives that are worth living.